W9-CQZ-979

Hunting

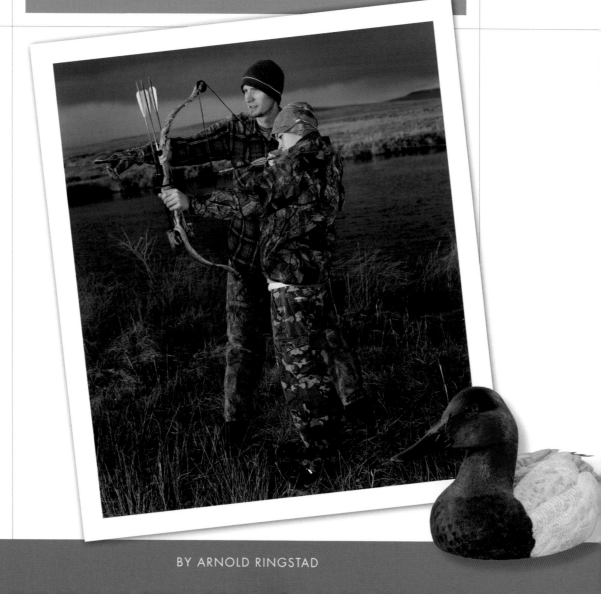

BY ARNOLD RINGSTAD

Published by The Child's World®
1980 Lookout Drive • Mankato, MN 56003-1705
800-599-READ • www.childsworld.com

Acknowledgments
The Child's World®: Mary Berendes, Publishing Director
Red Line Editorial: Editorial direction
The Design Lab: Design
Amnet: Production

Photographs ©: Shane W Thompson/Shutterstock Images, cover
(center), 1 (center), 16; Shutterstock Images, cover (top right),
cover (bottom right), back cover (right), back cover (bottom), 1
(top right), 1 (bottom right), 3, 4–5, 6, 7 (bottom), 15; James
Pierce/Shutterstock Images, back cover (left), 9; Photosync/
Shutterstock Images, 7 (top); BrandX Pictures, 8; Photodisc, 10;
iStockphoto, 11; Steve Oehlenschlager/Thinkstock, 13, 20–21;
Ivanov Arkady/Thinkstock, 14; Lantapix/Thinkstock, 17; Nathan
Allred/Thinkstock, 18; GG Pro Photo/Shutterstock Images, 19

ISBN 9781626873315
LCCN 2014930668

Printed in the United States of America
Mankato, MN
July, 2014
PA02222

ABOUT THE AUTHOR

Arnold Ringstad lives in Minnesota. His cat is great at hunting laser pointer dots.

CONTENTS

EXCITEMENT IN THE OUTDOORS

Hunting is an exciting sport. There are many ways to have fun. Hunting helps people feel closer to nature. Hunters learn lots of

information about the animals that live in their area. They also learn about plants so they can blend in with the environment. Hunters who use dogs spend time with their pets.

The sport helps bring people together. Many families have hunted for generations. Hunting is a special tradition for them. Older family members teach young family members how to hunt. New hunters can learn how to safely use weapons from experienced hunters.

WHAT IS HUNTING?

Hunting is the activity of tracking and killing animals. Humans have always hunted. Early people struggled to survive. They used as much as they could of every animal they killed. Early hunters ate the meat of the animals they killed.

Early hunters used every part of the animal they killed, including the skin.

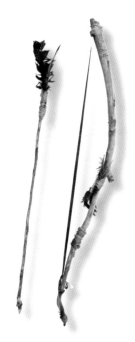

They made clothes out of skin and fur. They shaped horns and bones into tools.

Early hunters used sticks and stones. They later sharpened sticks into spears. Hunters invented bows and arrows. These tools let them kill prey from far away. A few hundred years ago, guns were invented. Guns allowed people to hunt from even longer distances. Today, most people use guns or bows and arrows to hunt.

Hunters have used bows and guns for hundreds of years.

PLACES TO HUNT

People hunt in many different places. Hunters pick a location based on what they want to hunt. Deer and bears are often found in forests. Ducks live near water. Cougars can be found in rocky areas. Hunters must bring different gear to different locations.

There are two basic kinds of land: public and private. The government owns public land. Anyone can hunt there. Private land is

Hunters enjoy scenic mountains, green forests, and the calm shores of lakes and rivers.

owned by someone. Hunters who want to hunt on private land must get permission from the person who owns it.

Hunters can only hunt during certain times of the year. In the United States, state governments choose when hunting can take place. Those periods of time are called seasons. Seasons are often picked to protect animals when they are breeding. It is only legal to hunt animals when they are in season. Seasons keep hunters from killing too many animals. All hunters must follow hunting season rules.

Hunters can only hunt deer when the animals are in season.

BIG AND SMALL GAME

People hunt two types of land animals. The first is big game. In the United States, this includes large animals, such as deer, moose, and bears. Different big game can be found in other countries. In South Africa, people hunt elephants, lions, and giraffes.

Black bears are considered big game.

The second type of animal is small game. This includes squirrels, raccoons, rabbits, and other small animals.

Size is not the only difference between big game and small game. Hunters use different weapons to hunt them. Big game often needs bullets that are big and fast. Small game usually requires smaller **ammunition**. Sometimes, hunting seasons are different for small game and big game. The season for small game is usually longer than the big game season. That's because there are more small game animals to hunt. There is less danger of hunting too many of them.

ELEPHANT GUNS
In the 1800s, hunters invented huge guns to hunt large animals in Africa. These huge guns were known as elephant guns. Elephants, hippos, and rhinos are often too big to hunt with normal guns.

Many hunters shoot small game, such as squirrels.

HUNTING BIRDS

Big game and small game are not the only animals people hunt. People also hunt birds. Waterfowl and upland birds are two popular kinds. Waterfowl are birds that live near water. Ducks and geese are waterfowl. Upland birds often live in open fields. They include quail and pheasants.

Hunters sometimes have special helpers for hunting waterfowl and upland birds. They use dogs that are trained to hunt. The dogs stay quiet. Hunters don't want them to scare the birds away. Dogs search for birds. Then, they point them out with their noses. After hunters shoot, the dogs run to the birds and bring them back.

WORKING DOGS

People have hunted with dogs for 20,000 years. When people started using farms to grow food, some dogs helped herd farm animals instead.

Dogs make excellent bird-hunting partners.

GUNS AND BOWS

A hunter's most important tool is his or her weapon. Most people use some type of gun. Hunters use two main kinds. **Rifles** are used for hunting big game and small game. These guns shoot one bullet at a time. The **barrel** of the gun has a spiral shape on the inside. This makes the bullet spin as it leaves the barrel. Spinning makes the bullet travel far and straight.

Hunters use **shotguns** for hunting birds. Instead of one bullet, these guns shoot many small **pellets**. The pellets spread out after they leave the gun. This makes it easier to hit a moving target, such as a flying bird. Shotgun pellets do not do as much damage as rifle bullets.

Use shotgun pellets for hunting small animals.

This makes shotguns useful for hunting small animals, such as waterfowl and upland birds.

Some hunters use bows and arrows to hunt. This can be more challenging than using a gun. Hunters must be strong to pull back the arrow. They need practice to make sure they can shoot accurately.

CROSSBOWS

A special kind of bow is like a mix between a gun and a bow. It is called a crossbow. It shoots arrows like a bow. However, hunters pull a trigger to fire it rather than pulling back an arrow.

Some people hunt with crossbows such as this one.

STAYING HIDDEN

Hunters have many tools to make hunting easier. Some of these tools help them stay hidden from the animals they are hunting. Wearing **camouflage** clothing is one way to stay hidden. This clothing has patterns and colors that blend in with the environment. For example, camouflage clothing used in

Wear camouflage to blend into the environment while hunting.

a forest is brown and green with a leafy pattern. The pattern makes it hard to see the hunter.

Many animals have good senses of smell. It is important for hunters to hide their scent from the animals they want to hunt. Special clothing can help keep a hunter's scent from getting out. Hunters also spray scents on themselves to blend in. In a forest, a hunter might try to smell like acorns or dirt.

Another way to stay hidden is to climb into the trees. Hunters use **tree stands** so animals cannot see them. Some tree stands are platforms attached to trees. Others can stand alone. Hunters find a place where they think an animal might walk by. Then they place the stand there and climb up. If an animal comes near, the hunter has a chance to shoot it.

Hunters use tree stands to stay hidden from animals.

HUNTING SAFETY

Hunting safety is extremely important. Guns and bows can be deadly if used incorrectly. Before going into the wilderness, you need to take safety classes on how to use a weapon.

Have an experienced hunter help you learn how to hunt.

First-time hunters should also have an experienced hunter help them learn. Special clothing can help keep hunters safe. Camouflage clothing hides hunters from animals. But it can also make it hard for other hunters to see them. One hunter might accidentally shoot at another. To stop this from happening, many states have special rules. Hunters must wear some clothing that is a special color. The color is called hunter orange. Hunter orange is easy for people to see. But deer eyes work differently. They do not see hunter orange the way people do. Hunters wearing this color can still stay hidden from deer.

HUNTER ORANGE
Deer cannot see as much detail and color as people. Hunter orange most likely looks brown or gray to them. However, turkeys and waterfowl have excellent eyesight. They can spot hunter orange. Many states do not require hunters to wear orange when hunting these birds.

Wearing bright orange helps hunters see each other.

FUN WITH HUNTING

Hunting can be fun because it combines old and new. Hunting traditions go back many years. Hunters use new technology that helps

Hunting is a fun way to spend time with friends and family.

them hunt more successfully. Hunting can be fun whether you use a traditional bow or a modern rifle.

Hunting is an exciting way to feel closer to nature. Hunting lets you experience how earlier people lived. Many hunters enjoy spending quiet hours in the wilderness. It helps them feel connected to nature.

GLOSSARY

ammunition (am-yu-NI-shun): Ammunition is objects shot from weapons. Bullets and shotgun pellets are examples of ammunition.

barrel (BAYR-uhl): A barrel is the part of the gun a bullet moves through. Rifles have barrels with spiral shapes on the inside.

camouflage (CAM-oh-flaj): Camouflage patterns have colors and shapes that blend into the environment. Hunters use camouflage clothing to hide from animals.

pellets (PEL-its): Pellets are tiny metal balls shot out of shotguns. Pellets spread out when fired from a gun.

rifles (RYE-fulz): Rifles are long guns that shoot one bullet at a time. Hunters use rifles to hunt large game.

shotguns (SHOT-gunz): Shotguns are guns that shoot pellets. Hunters use shotguns to hunt birds.

tree stands (TREE standz): Tree stands are platforms connected to the branches and trunks of trees. Hunters sit in tree stands to hide from animals.

TO LEARN MORE

BOOKS

Gross, W. H. *Young Beginner's Guide to Shooting and Archery: Tips for Gun and Bow*. Minneapolis: Creative Publishing International, 2009.

Lambert, Hines. *Hunting Moose and Elk*. New York: PowerKids Press, 2013.

Watkins, Sue. *Getting Involved! A Guide to Hunting and Conservation for Kids!* Long Beach, CA: Safari Press, 2010.

WEB SITES

Visit our Web site for links about hunting:
childsworld.com/links

Note to Parents, Teachers, and Librarians: We routinely verify our Web links to make sure they are safe and active sites. So encourage your readers to check them out!

INDEX